Computer Shortcuts

To Simplify Your Life

Aimee McPartlan

ACKNOWLEDGEMENTS

As with all of my books, I must first acknowledge my parents, grandparents and siblings for their love and support throughout my life. If not for their continued lack of technical knowledge, I would not have the skills needed to write this shortcut manual.

(I say that with love, of course)

I would like to thank my dear friend, Dr. Howard Jenkin, for the unique combination of ingenuity and lack of technical savvy that led to his request for a written computer manual in the first place.

I would like to thank Editor, Sam Attard, for not allowing me to publish the garbage I initially wrote.

I would like to thank my best friend, Jim Hill, for something.

Can't say what.

TABLE OF CONTENTS

Each time I go to my parents house for a home cooked meal, I go with the understanding that they need help with their computer. That's not to say that they wouldn't invite me over otherwise, but I'm the only one of the group that gets out of having to bring a sidedish. Nope, my contribution comes in the form of technical assistance. It's showing Mom how to attach the latest picture of her grandkids to an email or teaching Dad how to use spell check on a letter to a client. It is the same with my grandparents: dinner, pie, ice cream, socializing and then computer class. I love it! I love being able to wear the super hero cape for them every now and then, because they've been wearing one for me my enire life.

All of those computer questions got me thinking: do my friends do this with their parents and grandparents? So, I started asking around and the answer was an astounding, "YES!" It turns out that my generation and below, those of us who have grown up with computers, have quite a lot of wisdom to impart on our elder generations- at least when it comes to technology.

I am not a computer expert. My degree is not in anything remotely technical. But that's good; if you are reading this, you're not looking for something technical. Chances are, you're simply trying to avoid having to ask a kid you know, or a neighbor down the street (for the tenth time) how to send an email to an old friend or download pictures from your camera to your desktop. Right?

And by the way, we always go too fast and I know this. We click through five screens in lightning speed, step back and say, "See? It's easy." And even though you're still trying to figure out where the heck we started step one, you smile and say thank you, thinking that you may just go back to letter writing, snail mail and polariods.

Well you've come to the right place. I've compiled the most common questions I have received over the years from my parents, grandparents and their friends and put them into one easy place for you to reference. I can't guarentee that it will answer all of your questions. You may still need a Generation Y'er on standby, but my hope is that it will help.

Note: The shortcuts in this manual are for users who are running Windows 98, Windows XP, Windows Vista and Windows 7. Did you buy your computer before 2013? If yes, then keep reading.

DESKTOP -- The main computer screen that you look at all the time. The place where all of the icons are displayed.

ICON -- The little pictograms on the desktop that link to programs when you double-click on them.

LEFT-CLICK -- The left button on your mouse. You use this most of the time when navigating the programs on your computer or the internet.

RIGHT-CLICK -- The button on the right on your mouse. In many programs, clicking this button one time will bring up a menu with additional options. It can't hurt anything to try it.

START MENU -- Circular icon on bottom left of the desktop. Clicking on this brings up all of the programs installed on your computer. Take time to familiarize yourself with the start menu so that you are better able to locate things later.

WALLPAPER -- Another name for the desktop background (the picture you see as a backdrop of your computer screen).

DIALOGUE BOX -- A box that appears on the display screen to present information or request input. The dialogue box is usually temporary and disappears once input has been entered.

WINDOW -- An enclosed, rectangular area on your display screen. Within each window, you can run a different program or display different data.

TASK BAR -- The bar on the bottom or side of your desktop that is used to launch and monitor running applications or programs.

RIBBON -- A set of toolbars placed on several tabs and organized by functionality.

I want to...

Put a picture of my grandkids on my desktop so I can smile every time I'm on the computer:

Put your cursor anywhere on the open spaces of your desktop (not on an icon) and right-click. You will see a menu of options. Find **Properties**, usually the bottom choice. Under the background tab, look down where it says wallpaper. Choose from the list of preloaded images or click Browse and Open. Select a file folder on your computer that contains your pictures. You can choose if you want the image centered, stretched or tiled. These choices are solely aesthetic so you can play around with it and decide what you like best. You can also change the screensaver in this section by selecting the screensaver tab at the top of the dialogue box.

Find something I know I saved but can't remember where:

No problem! Click on the start menu (the circle shaped icon on the lower left corner of your desktop). You are looking for the search function. Depending on your version of Windows, the location may look a bit different but should still be in the same general area. Look for the magnifying glass or the word "search." Type a key word from the document or file you are trying to find. A list of results will open in a new window. Read through and double-click on the file you are searching for. If that doesn't work, go back to the search box and type in a different keyword in the file you are looking for and repeat the process until you find it.

Print something . . . but I can't find the icon:

You can print any page simply by holding down the **Control key** (**CTRL** on the bottom left corner) and the letter **P** (for print) at the same time. The dialogue box for print will appear.

Print something . . . but it won't fit on the page:

Changing the orientation of paper in your printer is an easy way to print things that are too wide for the portrait orientation (that's the regular setup) such as charts or spreadsheets. Simply command your computer to print by pressing **Ctrl** and **P** at the same time or by going to **File** then **Print** or by selecting the printer icon. Then select **Properties**. There will be an option to change the orientation of the paper to **landscape**.

Work on multiple things at once:

Figuring out how to make windows work will increase the ease of productivity. To flip through open windows, use the **Alt** and **Tab** keys together. The **Alt** button is on the left of the space bar. To arrange your windows, right-click on an open area on your task bar and a menu will pop up. In the menu you can choose to cascade, stack or display windows side by side.

Use the number pad on the right of the keyboard but it isn't working:

Make sure that the number lock key (above the number 7) is pressed.

Okay, you already know about using **Control** and **P** together, but there are many other keyboard shortcuts that will simplify your life:

First, locate the **Control** key (**CTRL**) on the lower left corner of the keyboard. Now, hold the **Control** key down while pressing the following letters to make different commands.

Control and **I**

Quickly write in italics by double clicking on the word or by holding the left mouse button down while you drag the cursor to highlight a phrase, then press **Control** and **I** to change the word to italics. Or, do this before you start typing to write everything in italics. Repeat it again to return to normal.

Control and **U**

Quickly underline something by double clicking on the word or by holding the left mouse button down while you drag the cursor to highlight a phrase, then press **Control** and **U** to underline.

Control and **B**

Quickly make something bold by double clicking on the word or by holding the left mouse button down while you drag the cursor to highlight a phrase, then press **Control** and **B** to make it bold. Or, do this before you start typing to write everything in bold. Repeat it again to return to normal.

Control and **F**

Looking for specific text on a page? Using this combo will open the "find" search function in any program.

Control and **C**

Copy text from any source by highlighting it with the mouse and then using this combo to copy it. Now what do you do with it? Read on my friend.

Control and **V**

Paste text that was just copied. This is helpful in word documents or emails or just about anywhere. The only problem is that when you copy from a source, the program will usually copy any formatting that went along with it as well. To avoid this and paste the text without formatting, use the following.

Control and **Shift** and **V**

Using this combo will paste unformatted text in most programs.

Control and **W**

Using this combo will close the current open window.

Control and **S**

In almost any file or program, pressing this combo will save the file. Use this frequently!

Control and **Z**

If only fixing mistakes in life were this easy: Use this combo to undo almost anything. It doesn't apply to just typing. If you delete or move a file by mistake, using **CTRL** and **Z** will put it right back where it was.

Control and **Y**

Redo anything you just "undid."

Control and **Backspace**

Delete a word that or words that you just typed instead of having to delete one letter at a time.

Control and **Home or Control** and **End**

Use one of these combos to move the cursor to the beginning or end of a document. These keys are located above the number pad on the right side of the keyboard.

Control and **Left Arrow** or **Control** and **Right Arrow**

Move the cursor to another word quickly instead of letter by letter. Holding down this combo will move the cursor left or right, word by word.

Control and Shift and N

Go incognito with this trick. Pressing this combo while browsing the internet will bring up an incognito window. Pages you view while in this window will not be displayed in the history on your computer.

Control and **Alt** and **Delete**

When your computer seems to be "frozen" use this combo to interrupt all processes. When the dialogue box appears with the options, choose task manager. Then find the program in the task manager that is not responding. Click on the program to highlight it and then click **End Task**.

Tab

The tab button is our friend. It allows you to quickly navigate through form fields instead of having to point to different fields with your mouse. For example: the next time you're entering your name, address, credit card info, etc on a website, try using the tab button to move between the spots where you need to enter information, it's a breeze.

Alt and **Tab**

Use this to cycle through currently open windows. This makes switching back and forth between programs or websites quick and painless.

Alt and **F4**

Quickly closes a program that is running instead of having to mouse over and click the "x" in the top right corner of the window.

Page Up and **Page Down**

Use the **Page Up** and **Page Down** keys to move a page up or down.

This is particularly helpful when browsing the internet.

Space Bar

Aside from its normal function, the **Space Bar** has a hidden bonus. When on the internet, hitting the **Space Bar** will move the page down. Hitting **Shift** and **Space bar**, will move the page up.

The next set of shortcuts have to do with using the Windows key on your keyboard.

The **Windows** key can be found to the left of the spacebar and has a picture of the Windows logo on it.

Windows and **Tab**

Switch through open programs quickly.

Windows and **E**

Open Windows Explorer without touching your mouse.

Windows and **M**

This is a neat trick to minimize all windows at once. To restore, use **Windows** and **Shift** and **M**

Windows and **D**

Another way to quickly return to your desktop.

Windows and **U** and **U**

Use this shortcut to shut down Windows. Hit the **Windows Key** and release, hit the letter **U**, then hit the letter **U** again.

EMAILS AND ATTACHMENTS

THIS is going to be a little tricky because there are so many different email providers and programs. Although there are many different formats, visually, they all have the same basic functions.

The first question we need to find out: Are you still checking your email by logging on to the internet (do you go to the internet, type in yahoo or AOL or some other email provider and then login to your email account)? If so, I have a suggestion for you: download an email client. **Wait!** Don't panic- let me explain.

There are two basic ways to read your email: on the internet- which means you've gone to your email provider on the internet (Yahoo, AOL, Gmail, etc) and then logged in to their site to read your email. The other way is by setting up an "email reading program" on your computer so that your email is always there, waiting for you, on your desktop and you don't have to actually go on to the internet to read it. Doing this can increase speed and productivity because your email is always there waiting for you. Plus, once you get familiar with it, I think you'll find that it's easier to use.

> Did you know that email has been around longer than the World Wide Web?

Some popular email clients are Microsoft Outlook, Lotus Notes, Pegasus Mail, Mozilla Thunderbird and Apple Mail but there are plenty of others. Personally, I use Microsoft Outlook. Some may consider that outdated, but I like it and it's the program that I've set up for my parents and they're fond of it; that must mean it's a winner!

If you've decided to set up an email client (think of it as a funnel that catches all of your messages and puts them in one easy place to read right on your desktop without having to log into anything) then continue reading for instructions. If you already have one, you can skip this.

This section goes a bit beyond what I intended for this book but the more I thought about it, the more I thought it was needed. Let's give it a try and if you find it more complicated than you would like, you may want to find someone to help you.

 In order to set up an email client, you need a few important pieces of information. You need to find out what servers your current email uses. You can find this info by logging into your webmail account (Yahoo, Gmail, AOL, etc) and searching for Configuration Instructions or Setup information. Most webmail providers have this readily available. You are looking for the following:

EMAILS AND ATTACHMENTS

Incoming Server

This is the server that receives and stores messages sent to your email account, accessed by the email client.

Outgoing Server (SMTP)

This is the server that sends email from your email account. Your SMTP server may require some additional settings but these are also fairly easy to find and configure.

> Hot Tip: If your mouse has a wheel in between the left and right buttons: use it! It's an easy and quick way to scroll through pages.

User Name & Password

Authentication credentials that you currently use to access your existing webmail account and messages.

Entering Account Information

If you are launching your local e-mail client (Outlook, Windows Mail, Thunderbird, etc) the "desktop funnel for your email," for the first time after you installed it you will need to enter the above information from your existing webmail account so your new email client knows where to "funnel" the email from.

21

I have included steps from some of the more popular email clients to help you in this process. Once you have completed these steps, you won't need to do it again and will find that sending and receiving email is much easier and faster from an email client.

Outlook

In top menu click on **Tools** and then **E-Mail Accounts** (some versions of Outlook may simply say **Accounts**).
In some versions of Outlook you may need to click on the **E-Mail** tab.
Click on **Add a new e-mail account** or simply **New** and then click **Next**.

Outlook Express/Windows Mail

Click on the **Tools** menu, click on **Accounts**, and then click on the **Mail** tab.

Click the **Add** button and then click on **Mail**.

Hot Tip: You can use ONE email client to funnel all of your email accounts into one place on your desktop

If you need additional or program specific step by step instructions, you can search the internet for your specific email provider.

EMAILS AND ATTACHMENTS

Each email Each email client has a slightly different layout but the general functions are the same. Spend some time exploring yours so that you are familiar with the layout. You need to find the functions to compose an email, reply to an email, forward an email, and, of course, send the email once you've typed it. I have a good friend who forgets to hit send after he spends time composing an email, and he then gets mad that he didn't get a response to his message that he never sent. Hopefully, if you forget to send, your message will be saved in the **Draft** folder, but why risk it?

After you've located the icon for a new message in your email client (usually by hitting a button that says **New** or **Compose**, or simply a plus sign (**+**)) enter the email address, subject, if desired, and body of the email.

Attaching a file or photo to your email is another important task. Simple! You will find a button that says **attach** or an icon with the picture of a paperclip on it. Click on that. A dialogue box will open allowing you to choose the file you would like to attach. Click through the file folders until you find the file or photo you want.

To select multiple files or photos, hold down the **Control** key and click the files or photos you want to include. Then click Attach.

If only attaching one file, you can simply double-click on the file or photo and it will automatically attach it and close the dialogue box. Once you familiarize yourself with your email client, you can create contact lists, personalized stationary and utilize the built in calendar that most email clients have. Go ahead, experiment and use trial and error (as long as you aren't in the middle of an important email).

Because Microsoft Word is so commonly used, I've included a section on the basics.

Microsoft Word is useful for an array of tasks such as letters, brochures, flyers, event invitations, homework assignments, reports, resumes, business letters etc. There's a template available for just about anything you want to do to make life easier.

Before we discuss templates, let's start with the fundamentals. Remember that, depending on which version of Word you are using, the layout will be slightly different. If you are using an older version of Word, prior to 2007, the top, left command is called **File**. This provides perhaps the most important menu of commands so you will need to familiarize yourself with it. If you are using a newer version of word, the **File** menu has been replaced by a circular icon called the **Office Button**. Both are located in the top left corner of the screen when Microsoft Word is open.

To make a new document:

To start a new document, simply go to **File** or **Office Button** and click **New**. This will bring up a dialogue box with options. Do you want a blank page to start on or do you want to start your project with a template? One of my favorite things is to start with a template and customize from there. Templates provide the kind of design and functionality you may want in your document but aren't sure how to make.

Let's say you want to make an invitation to a baby shower. Go to the **Office Button**, select **New** and then **Template**. Type in the keywords, "baby shower invitation." Word will search online templates and give you choices. Select the one you like by double clicking. You can then customize your invitation to fit your needs. This works with virtually any kind of document you could want.

SAVE YOUR WORK!

Before we go any further, let's go over the very important task of saving your work. I recommend that you do this often as you never know when something unexpected can happen to disrupt your project. This will save you the expense of repairing the window you throw your computer through when you realize your work is lost.

If this is the first time you are saving the document you're working on then you will need to tell the computer WHERE to save it. I recommend using file folders to organize your documents so that you always know where to find them. You can title the folders any way you wish or you can name them by person if you have multiple users in the same home.

Start with the **Office Button** (or **File**) and select **Save As**. Newer versions of Word will ask HOW you want to save the file before proceeding. Make your choice based on how you want to use the file in the future. Most likely you will chose to save as a regular word document. Another dialogue box will open and you will need to tell the computer WHERE to save your document. At this point you can put the document in a folder that is already there or hit the button to make a new folder. Once you've decided where to save it, name your document with something that will make it easy to find.

Now that you've made the initial save, you can continue to work on your document. When you've made progress on it, you'll need to save again. This time you can simply hit the icon that looks like a floppy disk (on the Quick Access Toolbar located on very top of screen) or go to the **Office Button** and click **Save** (not **Save As**). Word will save your document into the location you've already specified.

While You Work

Word offers many different options to customize the document you're working on and all are organized on the ribbon found on the top of the window (**Home**, **Insert**, **Page Layout**, etc) You can insert pictures, word art, clip art and text boxes plus many other things. The best thing is to play around with these functions as there are really too many to mention here. Take the time to start a blank document and experiment with different fonts or insert clip art or pictures from your computer. Most of the fun stuff you can add is found under the Insert tab on the ribbon (top of page next to the **Home** tab). There are also buttons on the **Home** tab to change font style, size and color and to change the layout of paragraphs.

Also note that if you want to utilize Word to do a mailing or print envelopes, a Mail Wizard can be found under the Mailings tab and will walk you through the process. **Don't Forget to Use Spell Check!**

Get a wireless mouse and keyboard... they will simplify your life!

It is very easy to make sure you're completing quality documents by using the spell check button. This will check spelling and grammar and can be found under the review tab on newer versions of word or under the Tools tab in older versions.

Ready to Print?

When you're ready to print your document you can use the **Control** and **P** shortcut we discussed or go to the office button and select print. It's a good idea to do a" print preview" first to make sure everything is correct and you have the desired layout. This will avoid wasting paper and ink. To do this, go to **File** and then select **Print**. Then click **Print Preview**.

Once you've commanded the computer to print, a print dialogue box will appear. Here, you can change the number of copies, change paper orientation (portrait or landscape) or command that only a section or a certain range of pages print.

Note: You can also use the printer icon found on the Quick Access Toolbar but only do this if you don't need to change any printer settings.

Holding the Control Button (CTRL on the lower left corner) and the letter P at the same time is the quickest way to print and is helpful when you don't see a print command on a page.

In addition to the keyboard shortcuts already mentioned, Microsoft Word has a few more:

You probably already know that to move or copy text from one place to another, you can highlight the text with your mouse, then use **Control** and **C** to copy it and **control** and **V** to paste it. But, did you know that you can double click or highlight what you want to move or copy and then drag it to where you want it to land?

Control and **Shift** and **D**

Okay, there aren't a lot of times that you will need this (Unless you _really_ like to emphasize) but if you want to double underline something simply double click the text, and press the combo **Control** and **Shift** and **D**.

Match Fonts (my favorite trick)

Have you ever gone insane trying to make the font from something you copied match the font you've pasted it into? Save your mental health with this trick: Highlight the non-matching text then hit **Control** and **Spacebar.**

Did you know that the world's first computer (the Z1) was invented in 1936?

IN SEARCH OF AN ICON

Your computer desktop is your command center. Customize it in order to simplify your life.

Do you have a website or a few websites that you frequently use? Do you have a program or file that you open on a regular basis? Create a desktop shortcut for it!

The quickest way to do this is to right click on an open area of your desktop. Select New from the menu that appears and click shortcut. A dialogue box will open. Click the program or file you want or type in a web address and then hit next or finish. Test it out- the shortcut should now be on your desktop.

You can arrange your Desktop Icons to suit your needs.

Drag the icons on your desktop if you want to change their location or you can sort them by right clicking on an open space on your desktop then click on Sort. You can sort icons by size, name or other options.

Delete unused icons to tidy up your desktop

Do you have icons on your desktop that you never use? Get rid of them. Right click on top of the icon that you don't use. Select delete and it will delete the icon. Note: Doing this will NOT delete the program or file, it will simply delete the shortcut to it.

A FEW MORE THINGS...

Wireless Home Networking

This manual wouldn't be complete without mentioning wireless internet. If you haven't already done so, consider buying a router (it could be built in to the modem given to you by your internet provider). Setting up a wireless router will enable you to connect any Wi-Fi enabled device to your home network.

Digital Cameras

Do you have a digital camera? Make sure that you are preserving your photos by transferring them from your camera to the computer. To do this, use the USB cable that came with your camera. Plug it into the camera and the other end into a USB port on your computer. Or, if your computer has a built in slot for an SD card (the tiny card that stores the images from your digital camera) you can insert the card directly into your computer. Doing either of these tasks should automatically prompt the photo software on your computer to open, giving you options for transferring your photos and saving them on your computer.

USB Ports

USB stands for Universal Serial Bus and is the industry standard for cables, connectors and communication devices. They are the small, rectangular ports on your computer where you plug in devices (keyboard, mice, digital cameras, printers, portable media players, etc).

Updates

Much like your car needs oil to run smoothly, your computer needs **updates.** Updates are modifications to software that can help fix problems, help your computer run more smoothly, upgrade to a newer version of a program or enhance your computer experience in one way or another. But you need to be mindful of where you are getting your updates. In other words, if while surfing the internet, a dialogue box comes up telling you that an update is needed for the page to display properly, that is not the best place to get your update. Here are a few important things to know:

The best way for Windows users is simply to be sure that the **Automatic Updates** feature is turned on. To do this, go to the **Start Menu,** click **System, Control Panel** and then click **Turn on Automatic Updates**.

In addition to Windows updates, your computer needs **Java** (a platform that runs various website applications and programs) and **Adobe Flash Player** (a program that adds videos and other interactivity to websites) to display properly. As mentioned earlier, you may get a message while on the internet that you need to update one of these programs. To do this, go directly to the **Java** website and **Adobe Flash Player** website instead of following links on a random webpage. This will ensure that you are downloading a clean version of these updates.

Another tool you can use to receive all of your needed updates at one time is a website called Ninite.com. **Ninite** is a trusted source for updates and is easy to use. Go to ninite.com to get started.

Don't Have Microsoft Word?

Libre Office is a free office suite that allows you to create documents and other projects online. Go to libreoffice.org to get started.

Backup Your Files

I will close with this very important rule: Back-up your files! Computers "crash" all of the time for a variety of reasons. You want to be protected. You have several options depending on the amount of files you have stored in your computer. For the average user, the most common methods of back-up are an external hard drive (available for approximately $65.00-$85.00 at any store that sells computers) or a USB flash drive, also known as a thumb drive. Flash drives are small and low cost; just don't forget where you put it once your files are on it!

If you find that the text you are typing in Word is typing over existing text instead of preserving it, hit the Insert button on the top right side of the keyboard. You do not want the insert function turned on, it will destroy your document!

Online back-up is becoming more common and can be done for $50-$100.00 per year on websites such as carbonite, Google Drive, iCloud, Mozy or SkyDrive. Personally, I prefer to keep my important files on something tangible that I can store in my home, but to each his own. **The moral of the story: Back-up your files and photos somewhere!**

Howard M Jenkin
Medical Foundation

Dr. Howard M. Jenkin rose from poverty to the top of his field in Chlamydia research, recognized worldwide. Dr. Jenkin has a PhD from the University of Chicago. His career included top positions such as: Professor and Head of the Department of Microbiology at the Hormel Institute, University of Minnesota, the top lipid research institute of the world, and consultant for the staff in four Departments of the Mayo Clinic.

Having lived 38 years in poverty, Dr. Jenkin knew that obtaining the highest education possible was his only hope of a bright future, free from the constraints of poverty. It took him 20 years of working two part-time jobs while going to school, but he finally achieved his goal: a PhD in Microbiology from the U of Chicago.

Dr. Jenkin retired in 1984, after 18 years as Professor and Head of Microbiology at the Hormel Institute, to Indian Harbour Beach where his desire to help others motivated him into action. In 2012, he founded the Howard M. Jenkin Medical Foundation which is now ready to fund the first round of scholarships. At the Howard M. Jenkin Medical Foundation, we welcome you to join us in doing our part to help impoverished students seeking medical, basic science and certain liberal art degrees to pursue advanced degrees and reach their full potential.

www.drhmjmedicalfoundation.org

Innovative Drain Technologies

Innovative Solutions for the Golf Industry

www.idtdrains.com

727-224-5246

Improving the quality of golf courses throughout the country.

NOTES

www.ingramcontent.com/pod-product-compliance
Lightning Source LLC
LaVergne TN
LVHW052126070326
832902LV00038B/3958